A Benjamin Blog
and His Inquisitive Dog
Guide

France

Anita Ganeri

Raintree

Raintree is an imprint of Capstone Global Library Limited, a company incorporated in England and Wales having its registered office at 7 Pilgrim Street, London, EC4V 6LB – Registered company number: 6695582

www.raintreepublishers.co.uk
myorders@raintreepublishers.co.uk

Text © Capstone Global Library Limited 2015
The moral rights of the proprietor have been asserted.

Edited by Dan Nunn, Helen Cox Cannons, and Gina Kammer
Designed by Jo Hinton-Malivoire
Picture research by Ruth Blair and Hannah Taylor
Production by Helen McCreath
Originated by Capstone Global Library Ltd
Printed and bound in China

ISBN 978 1 406 28110 1
18 17 16 15 14
10 9 8 7 6 5 4 3 2 1

British Library Cataloguing in Publication Data
A full catalogue record for this book is available from the British Library.

Acknowledgements
We would like to thank the following for permission to reproduce photographs:

Alamy: Action Plus Sports Images, 22, Angelo Hornak, 12, Carlo Bollo, 15, Directphoto.org, 17, Jean-Yves Roure, 14, John Kellerman, 4, LatitudeStock, 23, Oleksii Sergieiev, 7; Getty Images: AFP/Lionel Bonaventure, 18, Bloomberg/Caroline Blumberg, 25, M G Therin Weise, 11, Sylvain Sonnet, 16, Visions of America/Joseph Sohm, 10; Shutterstock: Gurgen Bakhshetsyan, 13, Iakov Kalinin, cover, Kiev.Victor, 6, macumazahn, 8, Neirfy, 27, Paul Stringer, 28, PHB.cz/Richard Semik, 9, Prochasson Frederic, 21, WDG Photo, 26, 29; Superstock: age fotostock/J.D. Dallet, 24, Robert Harding Picture Library, 19, Tips Images/Dino Fracchia, 20

Every effort has been made to contact copyright holders of material reproduced in this book. Any omissions will be rectified in subsequent printings if notice is given to the publisher.

All the internet addresses (URLs) given in this book were valid at the time of going to press. However, due to the dynamic nature of the internet, some addresses may have changed, or sites may have changed or ceased to exist since publication. While the author and publisher regret any inconvenience this may cause readers, no responsibility for any such changes can be accepted by either the author or the publisher.

Some words are shown in bold, **like this**. You can find out what they mean by looking in the glossary.

Contents

Welcome to France!

Hello! My name is Benjamin Blog and this is Barko Polo, my **inquisitive** dog. (He is named after ancient ace explorer, **Marco Polo**.) We have just got back from our latest adventure – exploring France. We put this book together from some of the blog posts we wrote on the way.

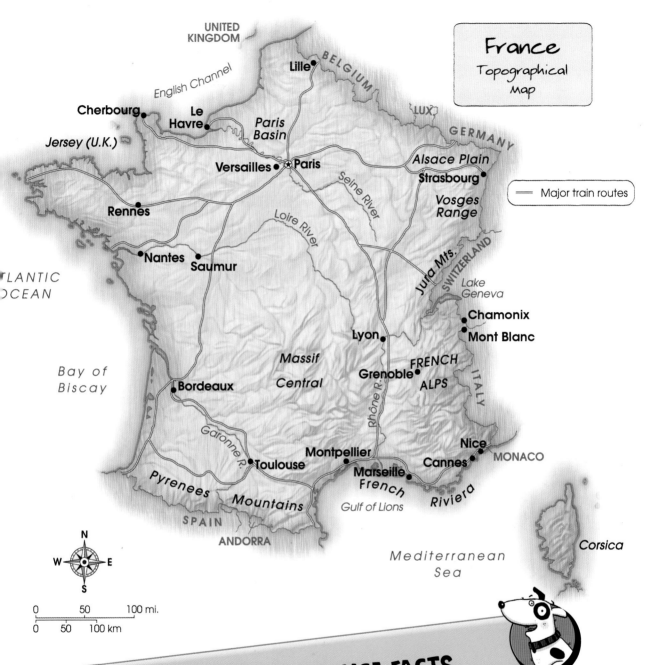

France
Topographical
Map

UNITED
KINGDOM

English Channel

BELGIUM

Lille

LUX

GERMANY

Cherbourg

Le
Havre

Paris
Basin

Alsace Plain

Jersey (U.K.)

Strasbourg

Versailles • ★ Paris

Seine River

Vosges
Range

Rennes

— Major train routes

Loire River

Nantes

Saumur

ATLANTIC
OCEAN

Jura Mts.

SWITZERLAND

Lake
Geneva

Chamonix

Mont Blanc

Massif

Lyon

Central

Bay of
Biscay

Bordeaux

Grenoble

FRENCH

ALPS

ITALY

Rhône R.

Garonne R.

Montpellier

Nice

Toulouse

Marseille

Cannes

MONACO

Pyrenees

French

Mountains

Gulf of Lions

Riviera

SPAIN

ANDORRA

Mediterranean
Sea

Corsica

N

W   E

S

0   50   100 mi.

0   50   100 km

BARKO'S BLOG-TASTIC FRANCE FACTS

France is a large country in Europe. It has coastlines
on the English Channel, Atlantic Ocean, and
Mediterranean Sea. On land, it is joined to Spain,
Italy, Switzerland, Germany, Luxembourg, Belgium,
Andorra, and Monaco.

Palaces and statues

Posted by: Ben Blog | 31 March at 11.45 a.m.

The first stop on our tour is the magnificent Palace of Versailles outside Paris. It was first built by King Louis XIII, who ruled France from 1643 to 1715. It was later changed into a palace by King Louis XIV. Now it has more than 2,000 rooms, so it is easy to get lost. I sent Barko off to find a guide.

BARKO'S BLOG-TASTIC FRANCE FACTS

Napoleon Bonaparte was a brilliant army general who made himself **emperor** of France in 1804. However, he was beaten by the British in 1815 at the Battle of Waterloo. No wonder this statue of Napoleon looks so cross!

Mountains, rivers, and beaches

Posted by: Ben Blog | 14 April at 7.56 a.m.

From Versailles, we headed to the Alps to climb Mont Blanc. It is the highest mountain in France at 4,807 metres (15,771 feet). If you do not like climbing, you can always go skiing or walking at the nearby town of Chamonix instead.

BARKO'S BLOG-TASTIC FRANCE FACTS

The Loire is the longest river in France. It flows for 1,020 kilometres (634 miles), from the Massif Central mountains to the Atlantic Ocean. It is famous for its **châteaux**, like this one at Saumur.

After a hard day's climbing, we needed a rest, so we travelled south for a little sunbathing. This stretch of coast is called the French Riviera, and it is famous for its sunny weather and sandy beaches. There are also beaches and sensational **sand dunes** along the west coast.

BARKO'S BLOG-TASTIC FRANCE FACTS

The Camargue is a huge **marsh** in the south of France, where the river Rhône flows into the sea. It is home to hundreds of birds, including pink flamingos, as well as herds of wild horses and bulls.

Big cities

Our next stop was Paris, the capital city of France. It is famous for the Notre Dame Cathedral, the Arc de Triomphe, the Louvre museum, and lots more besides. The best way to get around is by the underground, which is known as the Métro. I just need to work out which train to catch!

BARKO'S BLOG-TASTIC FRANCE FACTS

Marseilles is France's second biggest city and its main **port**. Each year, millions of tonnes of goods, such as oil, chemicals, plastics, and olive oil, pass through the busy port.

Bonjour!

Posted by: Ben Blog | 5 May at 11.23 a.m.

While we are here, I am trying to learn some French. It is going quite well so far. *Bonjour* means "hello" and *au revoir* means "good-bye." "*Je m'appelle Benjamin Blog. C'est mon chien, Barko,*" means "My name is Benjamin Blog. This is my dog, Barko."

BARKO'S BLOG-TASTIC FRANCE FACTS

Some countries in Africa were once ruled by France. Many people from these countries have come to live in France. These women are wearing traditional African scarves and clothing.

In France, children have to go to school between the ages of 6 and 16. These children are at an *école* (primary school). When they are 11, they go to a *collège* (middle school). Then, at 15, they move on to a *lycée* (high school). Older children sometimes go to school on Saturday mornings too!

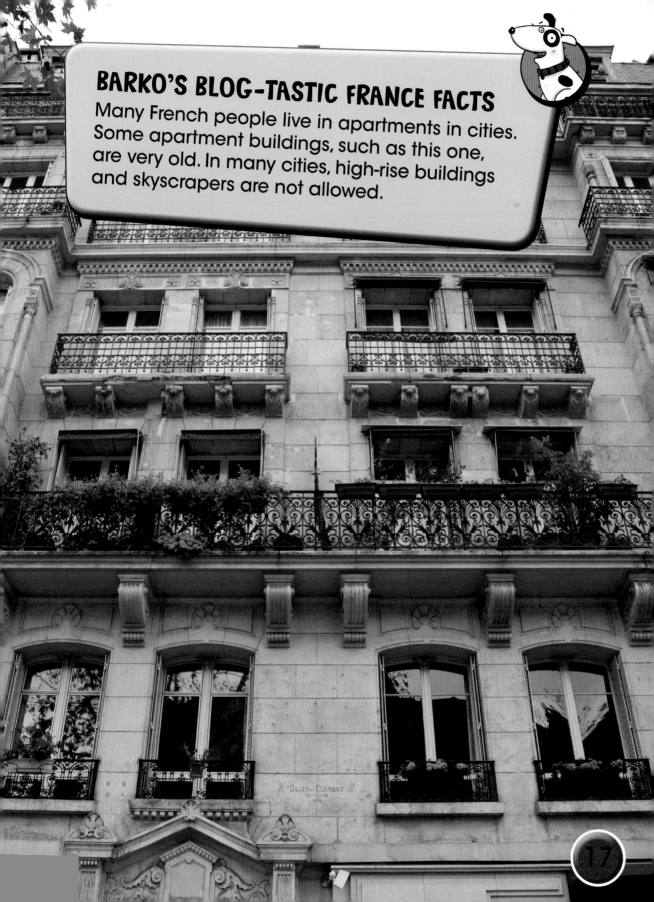

BARKO'S BLOG-TASTIC FRANCE FACTS

Many French people live in apartments in cities. Some apartment buildings, such as this one, are very old. In many cities, high-rise buildings and skyscrapers are not allowed.

Well, we are back in Paris for Bastille Day. It is a national holiday, and everyone is out celebrating. On 14 July 1789, an angry crowd attacked the Bastille prison in Paris. They were tired of being hungry and poor while the king lived in luxury. Afterward, France got rid of the king and became a **republic**.

BARKO'S BLOG-TASTIC FRANCE FACTS

Many French people are **Roman Catholics**. There are also many **Muslims**. Many come from countries in North Africa that were once ruled by France.

Lunchtime

Posted by: Ben Blog | 16 July at 1.15 p.m.

French food is famous all over the world, so we treated ourselves to lunch in a café. France is especially famous for its **pâté**, cooked meats, and cheese. People shop in supermarkets but also in local markets for fruit and vegetables.

BARKO'S BLOG-TASTIC FRANCE FACTS

Boules is a game that is played all over France. The aim is to get your boule (ball) as close as possible to a smaller ball, called the cochonnet (jack). For some reason, the players get really annoyed if I run off with any of the balls!

From farms to factories

These **vineyards** in Bordeaux grow grapes, which are made into wine. French wine is world famous, and about 8 billion bottles are produced each year. Farmers also grow fruit, wheat, olives, and sunflowers. They keep sheep, pigs, and chickens. Some raise cattle for their meat and milk.

AIRBUS

BARKO'S BLOG-TASTIC FRANCE FACTS

Thousands of French people work in high-tech factories. This factory in Toulouse builds the Airbus 380 – the world's largest aeroplane. French factories also produce around 131,000 cars every month.

And finally ...

For the last stop on our trip, it was back to Paris. Here is a photo that Barko took of me in front of the amazing Eiffel Tower. It was built in 1889 from over 9,000 tonnes of steel. The tower is 324 metres (1,063 feet) tall, and I am taking the lift to the third level for a breathtaking view of the city.

Find out more

Books

France in Our World (Countries in Our World), Camilla de la Bedoyere (Franklin Watts, 2013)

France (My Country), Annabelle Lynch (Franklin Watts, 2012)

France (A World of Food), Kathy Elgin (Franklin Watts, 2010)

Websites

kids.nationalgeographic.com/kids/places
The National Geographic website has lots of information, photos, and maps of countries around the world.

www.worldatlas.com
Packed with information about various countries, this website includes flags, time zones, facts, maps, and timelines.

Index